Stage Left

Miriam D. Dufer

Copyright © 2007 by Miriam D. Dufer

All rights reserved. No part of this book may be reproduced or transmitted in any form or by any means without expressed permission by the author.

ISBN 978-0-6151-4796-3

Cover Art: Ballerina dreams by Zina Seletskaya. Agency: Dreamtimes.

Prelude photo: "Getting Ready" by Paul Butchard. Agency: Dreamtimes.

Interlude image: Old Violin with Music Sheet by Gino Santa Maria. Agency: Dreamtimes. *Cota Image*, Ballet Shoes by Billie Muller. Agency: Dreamtimes.

Final Photo: *Ballet Ballerina in Pain* © Billyfoto | Dreamstime.com

Dedication

To my daughter, Youngsun Kim, may the dance always be in your heart and to my husband, David, may our hearts always yearn to dance with each other

Also by Miriam D. Dufer

Ask your bookseller for those you've missed

The Image and Identity of the Black Woman in the Poetry and Prose of Toi Derricotte

Confessions and Other Strange Impulses: A Book of Poetry in Two Acts

Stage Left

Table of Contents

Prelude

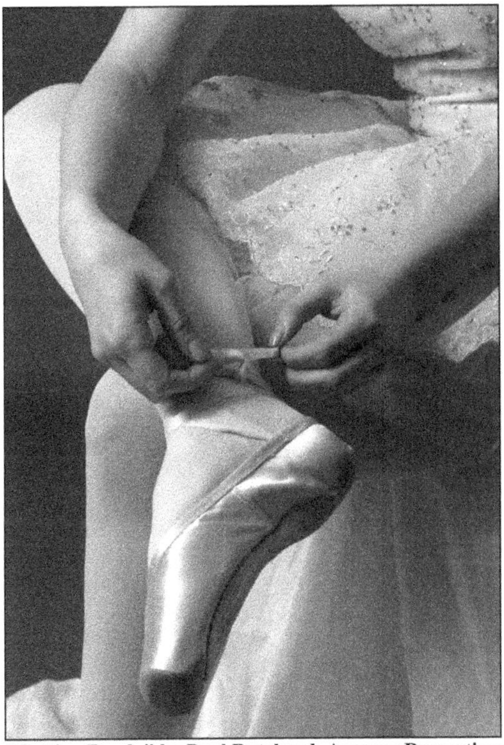

"Getting Ready" by Paul Butchard. Agency: Dreamtimes.

Eavesdropping

Snuggling behind a thick, insipid wall,
Hiding so mother couldn't see me,
I heard Mrs. Grebinski say
Mother should send us away.

My brothers and sisters cried as I
Told them and on a map of the world,
We planned our escape.

Penny wanted to go to Madagascar, Don chose Peru, and the others couldn't read
Yet and said they'd follow.

My callused heart wept for none
Of them. I planned a solo flight.
Lying in my twin-sized bed, crying
Into my purple pillow, I was already gone, alone

Woman Bigot

The woman who is a bigot
Is far worse than any God's fury,
Except her match, her gentleman,
Who really is Mr. Man.?

Belladonna

Deadly nightshades hide poison deep inside
Their ruby bell-shaped flowers and cradle blackberries.
A curious passer-by picks and nibbles on
Deadly nightshades that hide poison deep inside
Their ruby bell-shaped flowers and cradle blackberries.
A curious passer-by swallows and is gone.
Deadly nightshades hide poison deep inside
Their ruby bell-shaped flowers and cradle blackberries

Lady in Waiting

I won't be stagnate, waiting
For Prince Charming
Later to find he's
Really the wart on the frog's ass.

I've grown roses in my eyes
To see Adonis, flawless, statuesque
Perched upon the highest hill yet I
Feel disappointment when I met him
In human form

I won't be stagnate, waiting
For Prince Charming
Later to find he's
Really the wart on the frog's ass.

The Adonis in my mind is
Real and I can't let go, I cry ladylike lakes of tears,
Shaded by a cheeky grin.

I won't be frozen waiting
For my sweet Prince
Only to find him wanting.

Sources of Madness

The toilet seat left up, the door left unlocked while we sleep,
the traffic light that takes too long, the line at the check-out counter that never moves,
the soaking wet rug in the bathroom, the empty milk jug in the refrigerator,
the cold wet towel lying on the bed spread, the screaming silence in my head,
the salesgirl following me around the store asking, "Can I Help You"?
knowing full well that if I needed her help, I'd ask.

Nelly and Frances

Detest the rest soap and echo Nelly stand
On legs so spirited from tobacco
Frances,
The echo of debutantes impressed
Cold pens and needles pair balls rare and fruitful.
Rest now, do tell and leave me alone with romance
Dig low the love the vested Mr. John
Ten errors of ecstasy, crazy sense in pain
Germs and torn scoffing columns
Stand Nelly echo and soap the rest detested
Tobacco from spirited legs on Frances so
Impressed debutantes of Echo the
Fruitful and rare balls pair needles and pens cold
Romance with alone me leave and tell do now rest
John Mr. vested the love the low dig
Pain in sense crazy, ecstasy of errors ten
Columns scoffing torn and germs

Listen

Overture
building and building
Pianissimo and fade
Mano sinistra, Mano destra
Left and right and left and right
Passacaglia
Listen now

The Quarterback and the Majorette

You were my crush.
I knew you although we spoke rarely
A word. In my mind's eye
I saw me in your arms, feeling
Your heart beat and pulsing
Boyhood growing into man jeans.

You were my crush.
I found your number in the phone book and
Called every night and if you answered,
I'd hang up. If you didn't, I'd ask for Roger
or Brenda or some lone name.

You were my crush.
I'd sit on the band bus, with hot rollers in my hair, set for teasing
and poofing and hairspray, concentrating
on my twirling routine and hoping I'd twirl perfect for you. I
wanted you to watch my flawless finger twirls and splendid smile
brought on by the Vaseline spread
on my teeth.

You were my crush.
You had no idea how
On the bus ride home from the
Football games I lounged in the bus
Seat and watched movies of you and me
In my mind.

You were my crush.
I felt at home with you. You were my
comfort and desire.
The scenes changed from week to week
But our plot remained constant.
You wanted me. I wanted
You and we were together.

You were my crush.

The bus would stop in the parking
Lot near the band room. My mother
Would be waiting to take me home. I'd
Take off my green and gold fringed majorette
Uniform and soak my swollen feet, swollen
From marching at half time in those long
White majorette boots.

Out of the uniform, I was me again, swollen
Feet and all. I was sixteen and you were seventeen.
I had never been man spoiled and dreamt of giving you
My wine of womanhood. I was sixteen, a majorette, and
You were still my crush.

Conundrum

Enigma
mystical, cryptic
perplexing, baffling, bewildering
obscure, ambiguous, spiritual, magical
abiding, dangling
mysterious, secret
parable

Legends and Legacies from Grandma

Never put a new pair of shoes
on the kitchen table. It will surely
taint the atmosphere and someone,
chosen by the spirits, will get sick and
maybe die.

Bad luck comes to those who
enter one door and leave through
another.

Same thing with a bed, from
the side you enter you had better exit
less you want bad luck to rest with you.

Never give a gift of pearls. From the sea they come
and to the sea you will go if you give a gift of pearls. They are to
be inherited if the watery grave is to be escaped.

Good luck comes to those who decorate the window sill with shiny
golden coins on New Year's Eve. Tails are trailing badly all year
long.

Never put a hat on the bed. Someone you know will surely be
waking up dead.

Same thing goes for drinking sweet milk and fish; the two don't
mix unless you have a death wish.

Hold your breath when passing a cemetery or some roaming spirit
will jump your bones quite contrary.

Steppin' on graves is nothing
you do, the dead are living there so watch what you do.

Never take an all over bath when in the womanly way. Wash just
what you need washin'. This will

Keep you alive.

Everything that glitters ain't gold, child.
Fools gold fools a fool every time.

Experience is an expensive school and
a fool can learn from no other.

Never go to a funeral if you are with child for the spirits will
kidnap the soul of the unborn and let it loose in the wild.

If you dream about an ocean of fish,
pregnancy is upon someone you know.

If you dream of death, its right the opposite. A new life is comin',
waiting on the old.

Never reveal a dream before sunrise; less you want it to come true.

If your ear is burning, then someone is talking about you.
To determine whether what they are saying is good or bad,
remember this rhyme, - Left for love, Right for spite!
Legends and legacies of times gone by, I remember
the tales of Grandma and know that I
remember.

On List Making

The magnetic paperclip holder,
The scotch tape twins,
The black mouse, the sorority figurine in a box,
The black wool beret, Japanese dragons with a feather in the mouth,
Business cards jammed into the rolodex
Like tissue in a young girl's bra
On the night of her first date.

The Sound of Violent Voices

Noise and quiet
Serene, Uncomfortable
Deafening, Invigorating, Sedating
Clamor, Calm, Codswallop, Clerisy
Frustrating, Calculating, Liberating
Whimsy, Astucious
Nonsense and intelligentsia

Boychild

I remember the scene
Of the woman drowning her son because
Her husband was a son of a bitch. He brought
His whore home, parading the circus freak in the
Middle of the living room.

I remember wondering…what would drive a mother
To speed down the highway of desperation and
Drown her boychild?

As the boychild's head submerged under the water,
His nose protruding out like a submarine's periscope,
The nostrils began to fill and flood and sink him down.
Oh, how the bubbles rose to the surface and danced
And skipped and I was amazed.

As the boychild's plump modest body struggled and kicked
To grab a gasp of breath and breathe one last flash of
Life, I wondered…how she can watch her hands hold her
Boychild's house as his soul floats above her and forgives.

As the boychild's limp little body acquiesced to the strength
Of her hand, I hoped this would release her from her hellish
Prison and teach her husband…what?
The boychild is gone and she is alone and her husband
Is still with his whore in the bedroom.

Blissless Banter

I am weary and vexed
I dress in hand me down hope that hides the war torn spirit
I need to be renewed and cleansed and dried with a fluffy towel
I am related to the fallen but I try to disinherit them and not be an heir
I vacation in the bosom of blissless banter
My job is desperate and desolate
I desire peace and home to lay my weary head.

Interlude

Old Violin with Music Sheet by Gino Santa Maria. Agency: Dreamtimes.

Holding Hands

Most of the lovers on the street hold hands
And glance and sigh at my aloneness
Oh, to have someone and someone me
Or at least know the feeling of sweaty hands.

The Duomo

Firenze

I have been here for two days.
Yesterday, when I got to the stazione Campo di Marte, I
went to the window to call for a taxi. The man at the window,
Tall, dark, and Roman, smiled at me and said, *Ciao.*
You must have dinner with me, he said in his best English.
It was flattering and my knees were shaking and knocking.
Knock Knock Knock
Massimo….Massimo he was called and my inside voice
Screamed *Belllisomo Massimo!!!*

He asked if we could meet at the Duomo at 11: 30 p.m.
I said yes.
Tick Tock Tick
The knocking knees started again and would not let my
Feet move out the door. My mind wondered what would
Have, could have happened, if I had made it to the Duomo

Dream Sequence

There he is
I close my eyes
So they won't spill over
And scratch my puffy cheek.

I can say he sees me
And his passion swells
Deflated by the question
In my eyes

I can imagine his arm
Around me with hand
Tap, tap, tapping my breast
Feeding my ravenous rage.

I can say he is there
And I am his and
He says my name
How loud he screams

There he is
I open my eyes
So they can breath
The air that carries him.

I can feel his fingerprint
Disappearing into the bend
Of my arm while I
Lip him on the back of his neck

I can touch his name,
Dare I not,
There it is
I said it.

I can feel his words

Passing lips so powdery
Puffed and pouted
Drinking me down.

There he is
He sees my eyes
Red and blinking

Shaded from the rainfall.

I am here
Open and closed
Entering his heart-space
I can't say he knows me.

But that's not it.
Not at all.

Enigmatic

This is the poem that breathes
in the pen and ink of the notebook
that wears the veil of understanding
because I shadow the true meaning
because I illuminate the in between

And when crying over the words
I feel damp and crowded
this is the poem that breathes and pauses
in eternal freedom
just like the magazine

Grandpa Black Bear

I told Grandpa that it was my birthday.
He smiles at me and lowers his corn-cobbled piped.
He turns his back to me but I peek around to see
His hands, long and thin
reaching into his gray back pocket
To get his bulging wallet
Fingers pass over the twenties
and glide gleefully passed the tens
He grins
Turns around and
Hands me a one dollar bill
And says…
"Hold a dollar 'til it hollers"

Even at fifteen years old,
I knew this was generous for him.

At Carnivale 2000 in Venice

Fat Thursday
The butcher slaughters the bloody bull
And twelve pigs before
The Doge.
Faces in masses gathering in the squares,
Some smoke hash and the smell swallows
My nose in one big gulp.
Bongo drum drummers drum a pulsating rhythm
Beat, beat, beat
I dance and trance into another and another
Afro-Caribbean beats on the streets of the ancient
Roman Empire, Caesar's specter takes fancy flight around
And around, bouncing over horny lovers in gondolas.
Fire twirlers, spinning, throwing, entertaining crowds
As they stroll from bridge to bridge as firecrackers pop
Incessantly.

Self-Worship: A Response to a Compliment

I read your letter and thought

how peculiar this all is.

You admire my pink aura, pulled tight

with schizophrenic shadows.

My dead leaves are wet with draught,

singing with hazy phantoms.

The grotesque guilt I bought

Can not be sold, not even with coupons.

I have my shit together? Right.

The peculiar smell of organized and obsessed feces

neatly tucked far from fright.

You look up to me with sister's might

And awe of urine scented roses.

I want to be all that you see

For you, for me, by you, of you

But my self-worship of the guilty god

won’t let me

Be me.

Blooming Death

Mother, your flowers in the attic are blooming to death.
Their sunless shrivel whimpers in the weedy willows of shadows and secrets.
Mother, their lavender hue is fading and the need to suckle from your honey breasts.
Mother, your flowers in the attic are blooming to death.
Their rotting roots drink dank and stinky still water.
Mother, their sweet is starting soil is sour and their souls beckon for death. Why?
Mother, your flowers in the attic are blooming to death.
Prune them and show them the sun and share your secrets; they will understand.
Mother, their bulbs are burning, blazing for your touch.
Teach them your
Madness so they can wallow in the willows with you.
Mother, your flowers in the attic are blooming to death.
Smell them.

The Merriment of Writing

Muses merrily roam

the soft greens and pierce

the poet

with music and laugh.

Like a vagabond

warming himself

by the warming fire, fueled

by gas and copies of Shakespeare's

sonnets, the pale

rhyme rests

in the autumn season

and the muse

have tints the woodland.

Sudden delight shall meld

the muse

with the poet by chance

and delay the blank

page.

The Boulevard

University Boulevard seemed so long
To me when I was four years old. Peering out of the window of the speedy Gremlin,
There goes Denny Chimes, ding dong, ding Dong, the quad, to me, it went so fast.

I want to go there when I grow up, Mommy.
She smiles and says: Baby, you can. You can go anywhere you want.
I smiled.

University Boulevard seemed so long
To me when Bear died. The funeral procession was backed up all the way to the bridge over the Black Warrior. I watched it on t.v.
We were out of school that day.

University Boulevard seemed so long
as I walked from the quad back to the
dorm. The dorm sleeping next to Foster Auditorium. The auditorium where George stood strong in the door to keep out the wrong kind.

The wrong kind.
The wrong kind spat at the girl walking in front of me one day on the way to class.

Now when I go back and sing my
Alma Mater, I know that the wrong kind is
still around but the Boulevard doesn't seem as long anymore.

Depression

Wandering mind
Creating haze and shadows
Tears dancing and twirling
With fire, the face
Twitches without control
- depression -
Control without twitches
Face the fire with
Shadows and haze creating
Mind wandering

Waiting Makes Her Crazy

Mother waits
to leave husband
waiting makes her crazy
and the anxious pills do not help
anymore

In the Closet

In the closet,
behind the stack of fancy
shoe boxes, under the brown
mink jacket on a pastel pink satin
hanger, the white hood and robe
stood mocking Grandma as she
cleaned the bedroom of the nicest
white man she ever knew.

On Swimming Butterfly Wings

He loves
to say nothing
on swimming butterfly wings
and so nothing is what he says
to me.

Still Wind

Wind Stills
Nothing moves here
Isolated in stiff air
Frozen til my eyes open wide
Fantastic dream world

Principessa

Principessa is what you called me when you came
Into my frozen cocoon.
I remember the ice on the orange blossoms and
the fragrance of eucalyptus
and the salt on your lips and the
smoothness of you colossal needle
pricking away until the juicy nectar came.
Principessa is what you called me when you came
to awaken the dead and decaying lady in waiting.
She almost didn't recognize you or respond to
your invitation to be reborn.
She was hypnotized by what was supposed to be and
vexed by what was not.
I remember a garden of palm trees
and how erect they stood as we
promenaded passed them and I knew
that I was who I was meant to be but
You already knew that and we knew
Together.
Principessa is what you called me when you came
and introduced me to myself and I
remember.

Coda

Ballet Shoes by Billie Muller. Agency: Dreamtimes

Heart-Space

I am here
Open and closed
Entering his heart-space
I can't say he knows me.

But that's not it.
Not at all.

The Tortured Mind Lies on the Pillow

The tortured mind lies on the pillow,
Blessed by saints and guarded by falling angels;
Rest, rest and cloud the window.

Voices creep 'round like weeping willows,
Purple and green morning glory petals;
The tortured mind lies on the pillow.

Angels falling restless behind the shadows,
Saints dust honeysuckles gold at angles;
Rest, rest and stare out the window.

Eternal sounds shimmer sweet and hollow,
Quiet noise shouting thundered thoughts tangle
The tortured mind lying on the pink pillow.

Shouts, whispers, motionless memories of sorrow,
Topography of a tortured mind is mangled.
Rest, rest and cloud the window.

Voices spring silver and smile like sunflowers,
Whispers, shouts from multiple angles;
The tortured mind lies on the pink pillow;
Rest, rest and cloud the window.

Protocol in Dealing with the Dead

People say it is wrong to speak ill of the dead.
But what if they lived lives of dread?

The man who never ever said a kind word or helped a friend,
Who abandoned his children and wouldn't speak to kin.

People say it is wrong to speak ill of the dead.
But what if they lived lives of dread?

The woman who was pregnant and smoked two packs a day
And her child finds it difficult to learn and play.

People say it is wrong to speak ill of the dead.
But what if they lived lives of dread?

The father who beat his son with his fists because his father did it
And now the son is a father and continues to hit.

People say it is wrong to speak ill of the dead.
But what if they lived lives of dread?

The old white man who shot niggers for sport
And soiled black women before he would court.

People say it is wrong to speak ill of the dead.
But what if they lived lives of dread?

The young black man driving by with a gun
Spraying random death and hitting a nun.

People say it is wrong to speak ill of the dead.
But what if they lived lives of dread?

The young white girl giving birth at the prom
In the bathroom she leaves traces of being a mom.

People say it is wrong to speak ill of the dead.
But what if they lived lives of dread?

The man who rapes the virgin on her way home from school

And now she's afraid all the time but tries to act cool.

People say it is wrong to speak ill of the dead.
But what if they lived lives of dread?

The white woman who says she was raped by a black man
But was really caught screwing a white man.

People say it is wrong to speak ill of the dead.
But what if they lived lives of dread?

The sister who slept with her sister's husband
And when asked "why?" answers, "it just happened."

People say it is wrong to speak ill of the dead.
But what if they lived lives of dread?

Scenes from a Day without Zoloft

Focus. Take the wash cloth,
        Put it under the warm running
Water, rub some soap on it
        And scrub your face. Focus.
Rinse your face by cupping your
        Hands and scooping up the water. Splash.
Repeat. Splash.

Focus. Use the bathroom. Stand
        In front of the toilet, pull your drawers
Down, sit down. Release.
        Focus. Release.

Focus. Open the book. Read the words on
        The page. Don't let them run together. Focus.

Pick up the phone. Say hello. Listen to
        The caller. Focus. Listen.
Focus.

February 16, 1995

"We Are Free to Risk"
- Toi Derricotte

the words you inscribed in my
copy of Captivity didn't mean
much to me then. It was, you
know, my first poetry reading,
well,
the first, by a poet of color.

you spoke. i listened.
you spoke. i agreed.
you spoke. i disagreed.
you spoke. i questioned.
you spoke. i felt.
you spoke and i felt like
the parishioner feeling convicted by
the preacher's fire and brimstone sermon. you
spoke and i wondered how you spoke
the secret searching in my heart for home.

you spoke. i thought how much you
resembled my mother and
wondered if she had your same experiences.
did she?
you spoke and i recalled a moment
in the grocery store when i tapped a
white woman on the shoulder and called her "mom." she turned
around puzzled faced and i said "sorry, I thought you were my
mommy" and then mom walked up, a light-skinned blonde with
hazel eyes.

you spoke and my spirit
shouted, "i know her!"
the words you inscribed in my
copy of Captivity didn't mean

much to me back then. years gone by
and i have pondered who I am.

a poet afraid to speak the truth yet
truth is all i know. .
a poet possessed by a writing spirit
that forces me to immortalize the
truthful fear and swallow it whole.

a poet who writes for the silenced
little girl who wanted to speak about
being different, feeling weird and out
of place. the little girl who read Nancy drew and listened to Mozart
and was picked on by the "popular" kids. the little girl that never
questioned her blackness until the other black kids did.

the words you inscribed in my
copy of Captivity means so much to me now.
now,
i am free to risk
risk to freedom am i
in risk i have found
freedom
to risk freedom is to be
free truly

La Vecchia Religione

Great Grimas, preserve the old ways in me.
Hear my beckoning voice.
My moon bowl is readied with
Small bowls of nine.
Tell of the Holy Strega, teach me her ways.
Glorious Horace, invoke your Canidia and make
her call down the moon, call down the fixed stars
and make them my playthings.
I am but a servant, hear me!
Great Grimas, preserve the old ways in me.
Nonna is no more and I
am left lonely. My pewter chalice
is empty. Conjure the west winds
so I may take flight over Palermo and pick one
ripe olive from the ancient farm.
I am but a servant, hear me!

Fear

Metal on metal
Speeding for death
Suffering in freedom
Glass breaking glass
Dodging ditches and
Leaping light poles
- fear -
Light poles leaping
And ditches dodging
Glass breaking glass
Freedom in suffering
Death for speeding
Metal on metal

God in Glory Knows

Auntie Letha always said,
"God in Glory knows I ain't had a drop".
Not a drop but a bountiful bucket of
merry muscadine wine or liquor filled to the brim.

"God in Glory knows I ain't had a drop".
A deacon don't want no woman who drinks merry muscadine wine
or liquor filled to the brim.
But the deacon's lips are muscadine moist.

A deacon don't want no woman who drinks.
A deacon beckons for a lady of lust and love
but the deacon's lips are muscadine moist of cheerful chastity.

A deacon beckons for a lady of lust and love.
Aunt Letha loathes the sober summer somber of cheerful chastity.
The muscadines ripen bright green and purple on the vine.
The passion fruit of Southern breeding.

Auntie Letha loathes the sober summer somber
And sips and sips and sips her drops away.
The muscadines ripen bright green and purple on the vine and in
the vineyard, the deacon sneaks a kiss.

Dry Bones

Jen sang and Michael flew down from

Heaven to applaud her. The choir, off key, sang loudly

But Jen's plump vocal chords made the sounds worthwhile
She sang

About the dry bones and gave them life and made me
believe. The

Dry bones praised the Lord and so should I. The dry
bones

Could not be silenced nor should I. The dry
bones

Made me believe, if only for that
day.

Sickness

Conflict in its purest form is a sickness.
Callous words, callous deeds, callous bullets
Find the callous and not so callous shell and
Burrow their heads through spongy flesh and
Chips the bone.

Peace in its purest form is a sickness.
Pretty words, pretty deeds, pretty politics
Find pretty and not so pretty people and
Tickle their pride through smiles and
Hopeful hodgepodge.

Love in its purest form is a sickness.
Lusty words, lusty deeds, lusty lovers
Find lovely and not so lovely loads
Of the liquid death and men sailing the sea of risky love.

The Poem's Prayer

Tell me your secret
I can keep it, you know I can
Do I have it?

I am your winter dance, your pirouette
With frenzied arms of melodies of the mandolin
Tell me your secret

Whisper loudly in my ear and I'll detect
If you are you or a charlatan
Do I have it?

I am your summer breeze, your frantic
Winged rainbow blowing under the sand
Tell me your secret

Mumble to me and I'll translate
The mixed up mess so foreign
Do I have it?

Yes, dear playful poet,
I will lead you by the hand
Tell me your secret
Do you have it?

Applause

There is
A peace in noise
When hands come together
With praise and smiles and
Clap

Stage Left

dance from the heart; The world

needs
needs a super champion, And

That That could
stop a force so meek That single

limited trap, The centre, in the
You You like the gift that That my burden,

my passion, my burden, my core,
Always try
it! It in

the use
of every waking day.
dance will never

find your blinded; And drive and drive
and Always has that

nothing can possess; in a
demi plie or

a force so beloved
Yet I
let it all feel

to miss the Dance,
Dance LITTLE GIRL

in
your winning
carriage

poetry in pointe
then down to be just and
legend...

Just to chance
I
twirl, leap and aerial

To the shoes lay alone, Arms wrapped
around their pale pink tutus.

Slow and
returns

lyrical movement. The

tutu The

feet in air. with
the knee followed
almost immediately by the height
of lyrical movement.

It
is an entrechat dix.
Fouette: Turning step Pirouette: Complete
turn out:
of the hip without
any strain

Amber Leaves

The leaves
needed a Season to change color in.

A Council of Seasons was convened. ... praised them and reveled
in the shimmering shower of gold and amber. ...
Behold the hair; it is nothing but poplar leave

Lusitania arise from the ashes of the conquered!

Invoking Nantosuelta

She of the Sun warmed Valley,

She of the Winding River

Lusitania arise from the ashes of the conquered!

The leaves
needed a Season to change color in.

Great Pyrenees lose your snow capped

Fortress and surrender the landscape of

Freedom, flow winding river strait to Gibraltar

Warmed by the sun and behold the hair of this

Valley

Lusitania arises from the ashes of the conquered!

Nantosuelta speak to the mountains and make them

Move away and let the leaves change color this season

Behold the hair; it is nothing but poplar leave

Take leave, take leave

And resume the shimmering shower of amber and gold…

Speak ashes of the conquered from the fertile soil of new

Lands and new people

needed a Season to change color in.

A Council of Seasons was convened. ... praised them and reveled in the shimmering shower of gold and amber. ...

Four treasures from the

Druid who lived to cry out beneath every king

is there or was there a protective

emblem against devils, ghosts or amber,

both lunar and stellar; a

cave called Sanid

near to the Admiralty.

Lies the pole of combat, the sword of light,

The cauldron of cure and the stone

Of destiny

My Beloved

My Beloved, I never told you how I truly feel
You probably think my heart is from steel
Never shall I kiss someone else's lips
After kissing you I have yet to come to grips

With our love combined everything is in reach
Meeting you for the first time, I was without speech
The moment I saw you my heart was sold
I dream that together we will grow old

Our life together has just begun
We fit together, like the moon and the sun
Eternal bliss is where I'm bound
Near you, everything is sound

All of you is what I need
I count the hours until my love is freed
This poem has come to an end
See you soon, my dearest friend

I Asked

I asked the Negro why it was brown
And it smiled and walked a bit
I asked the Negro why it was black
And it walked a bit further
I asked the Negro why yellow
And it smiled and kept walking
I asked the Negro to identify
And it changed like a chameleon
I asked the Negro to comply and conform
And it did and the movement seemed real but it wasn't quite normal
I asked the Negro why white
And they gave me a wink, very polite
I asked myself why does it matter
And the Negro of many colors disappeared
The man appeared
The woman appeared
And I kept quiet
And everything was perfect.

About the Author

Miriam Donyelle Summerville was born in 1970 in Alabama. An avid reader since the age of 4, the written word has been her passion and means of expression all her life. One of her early influences was C.S. Lewis' *The Lion, the Witch and the Wardrobe*, which she checked out of her elementary school library so many times that she lost count. She attended the University of Alabama and continued her study of English and writing, completing her baccalaureate in 1998. In 2002, she married David A. Dufer III. In 2005, she received her Masters degree in Humanities with a concentration in Literature from California State University Dominguez Hills. She is the author of *The Image and Identity of the Black Woman in the Poetry and Prose of* Toi *Derricotte* and *Confessions and Other Strange Impulses: A Book of Poetry in Two Acts.* She is currently living in Seoul, South Korea. When she is not writing, she enjoys spending time with her daughter Youngsun, whose love for dance inspired the theme of this collection. Visit her website at www.mdufer.com.

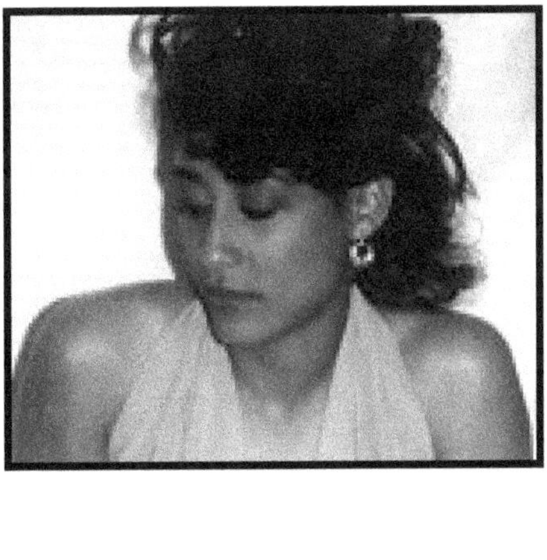

Ballet Ballerina in Pain © Billyfoto | Dreamstime.com

www.ingramcontent.com/pod-product-compliance
Lightning Source LLC
Chambersburg PA
CBHW032011080426
42735CB00007B/569
9780615147963